P9-CCJ-941

A Parent's Guide to the

BABY SIGNS®

Program

DEVELOPED BY
DR. LINDA ACREDOLO
DR. SUSAN GOODWYN

*The **Original** Sign Language Program for Babies*

Copyright © 2006 Baby Signs, Inc. All rights reserved. Printed in
China. No part of this book may be reproduced or copied in any form
or manner without written permission from Baby Signs, Inc.
Baby Signs®, BeeBo™, DiaperDoodles™, and all related titles, logos
and characters are trademarks of Baby Signs, Inc.
(800) 995-0226 www.babysigns.com.

CONTENT

WELCOME
FROM THE FOUNDERS

Dear Friends,

Welcome to the magical world of the Baby Signs® Program! You are about to start a journey that will change your parenting experience forever. Why? Because with signs literally "in hand," you and your baby will soon be enjoying a sense of connection and love that will make daily life immeasurably sweeter. That's a lot to promise, but having each personally experienced the joys of signing with our own children and grandchildren, and having received countless letters and emails from parents around the world, we know that what we're saying is true.

Babies are happiest when they can communicate with the people who love them the most — their families. Even when they are very young, they have lots to say and are looking for ways to tell others what they need, what they are feeling, or simply what they are intrigued by in the world. But without the ability to say words, they are at a loss as to how to get all these messages across. Now, with the revolutionary approach to communication you are about to master, your baby will be able to tell you all these things . . . and more.

Whether your baby learns one sign or one hundred signs, we are confident that you both will experience the reduced frustration that successful communication brings. And the good news for you as a busy parent is that using the Baby Signs® Program is simple. As we often say, it's as easy as waving "bye-bye."

Our own experiences with signing have given us more than just memories; they have also taught us many "secrets to success," a treasure trove of advice that has been greatly enriched in the years since by the contributions of thousands of Baby Signs® families just like yours. The Parent Guide to the Baby Signs® Program is designed to pass along as much of this information as we can so that your Baby Signs® adventure will be a success.

Happy Signing!

Linda Acredolo, Ph.D.   Susan Goodwyn, Ph.D.

CHAPTER 1
THE WORLD'S LEADING SIGN LANGUAGE PROGRAM FOR BABIES

Tiffany was in a hurry to get 17-month-old Molly dressed and out the door. On went the shirt, pants, and socks. So far so good. But then it was time for shoes, a task Molly had begun to enjoy doing herself. Tiffany, explaining the need for speed, quickly stuffed Molly's feet into the shoes and stood her up to get her coat on. As soon as she was on her feet, however, Molly plopped herself down again and started to cry. "Darn it!" thought Tiffany. "She's mad because I didn't let her put them on herself." Feeling frustrated, Tiffany was about to gently admonish her daughter when she saw Molly tap her index fingers together—the sign for "hurt." Knowing something must really be wrong, Tiffany took off the shoes and, lo and behold, discovered socks stuffed into each of the toes! No wonder they hurt! So, instead of scolding her daughter, Tiffany apologized, gave Molly a great big hug, and said a silent "Thank goodness!" for signing.

Stories like this are more and more common as parents around the world discover for themselves what a difference the Baby Signs® Program makes to daily life with their baby. Just as Molly was able to do, thousands upon thousands of babies from Brazil to China to Denmark to Russia are now using signs to let their parents know what they need long before they can say the words.

This particular story came to us from a Certified Baby Signs® Instructor in Maryland, one member of our rapidly growing network of Baby Signs® Instructors around the world. Like many of our instructors, Tiffany was so inspired by her own family's signing experience that she wanted to help as many other families as she could reap the same benefits.[1]

Our goal for this book is to introduce you to the Baby Signs® Program so that you truly understand what all the excitement is about and exactly how to start experiencing the rewards of signing within your own family. To this end we will devote a chapter to each of the following:

- WHAT the Baby Signs® Program is all about

- HOW we know for sure the Baby Signs® Program is good for babies

- WHY the Baby Signs® Program is so popular with families

- WHEN to get started

- HOW to choose and teach signs

- WHAT to expect along the way

We hope that by the end of the book you'll not only be eager to begin but also proud of yourself for having taken the first step toward a goal that is guaranteed to bring you great joy—gaining a window into your baby's mind.

CHAPTER 2
WHAT THE
BABY SIGNS® PROGRAM
IS ALL ABOUT

Why Sign Language for Babies?

There's nothing more heart-wrenching than hearing your baby cry and not knowing what's wrong. Unfortunately, until they can talk, babies are literally "at a loss for words" when it comes to telling us what's going on with them and how best we can help. They also don't have the words to tell us about all the things that fascinate them as they busily explore their worlds—the butterfly that flutters by, the bird that they see high in the tree, the dog that they hear barking down the street.

The problem is with the painstakingly slow development of the ability to produce words. To say even a simple word like "milk" or "juice" requires the intricate sequencing of a complex assortment of tiny muscles. Sure, babies can babble speech sounds from quite a young age. They entertain both themselves and us with their strings of silly syllables, sometimes making us wonder if they aren't actually speaking a foreign language! But babbling is just play. It's like randomly banging the keys on the piano, which produces sounds but not music. Likewise, moving from random babbling to saying "kitty" or "doggie" also requires learning precise movements of the tongue, lips, and all the other "equipment" that is called into action when we speak to one another.

Fortunately, babies are a good deal more adept at controlling the movement of other parts of their bodies, and that's where signs come in. They may not be able to reliably control their vocal cords, but they certainly can move their hands and arms. What's more, unlike the movements parents make when they say words, the movements they make when they model signs are easy to see. In fact, parents can even hold a baby's hand and gently help make the right movements.

BABY SIGNS® STORY
"Surprise! He's All Ears, Too"

Fourteen-month-old Henry and his 3-year-old brother, Chad, shared a bedroom. After Henry got tucked in, it was always Chad's turn for a cuddle with mom and a good book. For at least two weeks straight, Chad asked for the same book: Marvin K. Mooney *by Dr. Suess. One afternoon when Henry's mom was putting him down for a nap, Henry suddenly began making the sign for MOON. Mom didn't see any moons around, so she put him down on the floor, whereupon he went right to the bookshelf and —you guessed it— grabbed the* Marvin K. MOON-ey *book! Clearly, Henry had been enjoying the rhythms of Dr. Seuss too!*

Another of Mother Nature's Tools

When they first hear about teaching sign language to babies, some people think that it's a radical idea—that it means introducing something artificial into a baby's life. Nothing could be further from the truth! In fact, our research at the University of California, Davis in the 1980s demonstrated that most babies, in their eagerness to communicate, actually create at least one sign on their own. For example, we found babies using a panting sign for DOG, a sniffing sign for FLOWER, and a blowing sign for HOT, among many others. One day, while interviewing a mother for our study, we even witnessed a toddler walk in the room, tug on her mom's leg, and do a two-sign creation: panting + a knob-turning gesture. The mom immediately excused herself for a moment, explaining, "I guess the DOG wants to go OUTSIDE."

Here's another indication of how natural signing is: all parents teach their babies at least two signs without even thinking about it. We're sure you're no exception.

- Suppose your baby is about to touch something he's not supposed to. What do you do? Quite probably, you say a firm "No!" and shake your head back and forth.

- Suppose you want to tell your baby it's okay to touch something. What do you do? Quite probably, you smile, say a friendly "Yes," and nod your head up and down.

These two gestures, shaking the head for "no" and nodding for "yes," are actually signs. In other words, they are physical movements that stand for (symbolize) particular messages. All babies learn these two by imitating their parents—unfortunately, usually figuring out the "no" sign before the "yes!"

In addition, all parents, whether or not they have ever heard of the Baby Signs® Program, teach their babies another sign—a hand wave for "bye-bye." These three signs are so useful, in fact, that we continue to use them throughout our lives. What you'll discover for yourself, however, is that these three signs are just the tip of the iceberg. Babies are not just capable of learning many, many more signs, but are eager to do so.

The Baby Signs® Program: Our Sign Suggestions

The goal of the Baby Signs® Program is to make it easy for parents to fulfill this strong urge that babies have to communicate before they can talk, specifically, by providing babies with the signs that they can use most easily to express their needs, thoughts and feelings until they have words.

As you'll see, many of our Baby Signs® resources include specific signs for you to consider teaching your baby. Our choice of signs was not random or even based on just our own opinions. To make our selections, we called on colleagues familiar with child development, as well as parents in our research studies, to help us determine what 100 concepts would be most helpful for babies to be able to communicate about. Based on their recommendations, we selected 100 signs for inclusion in the Video Dictionary on the Welcome to the Baby Signs® Program DVD.

Most of the signs in the Baby Signs® Program are drawn from American Sign Language (ASL) because we believe that building a bridge to the Deaf community is a wonderful goal. A few are ASL signs that have been modified to make them easier for little fingers. A few other recommended signs are gestures that closely match babies' direct experiences, like blowing for HOT, pinching fingers as if picking up Cheerios® for CEREAL, and panting for DOG. In other words, *natural* signs.

A very important part of the Baby Signs® Philosophy, however, is that you are free to use whatever signs work best to help you communicate with your own baby. Signing is about communication, understanding, and intimacy between you and your baby. In the end, whatever signs you use, you are opening the world to your baby and opening your baby's world to you.

WHAT SIGNING PARENTS SAY

*We adopted our daughter from China at 11 months.
She understood some Chinese, but did not speak
Chinese or English. Anyway, it took about 3 months
working on 2 signs with my daughter, and finally
one day, she used one of the signs herself! I love
having my daughter tell me that she sees a flower,
a horse, a baby and that she is hungry or wants a
drink. She even says please and thank you!*

–Florida Mom

CHAPTER 3
HOW WE KNOW SIGNING IS GOOD FOR BABIES

Two Decades of Research

In a nutshell, we know that signing is good for babies because we've been conducting research on the topic for over two decades. As mothers ourselves, we were not about to promote something that might in any way hurt children. Fortunately, we were also researchers and, therefore, had backgrounds in both child development and research methods that made it possible for us to determine for sure what effects signing would have on children's development.

As you are about to learn, the Baby Signs® Program is the culmination of a systematic program of research conducted at the University of California at Davis. We were in charge of the work, of course, but we certainly couldn't have accomplished all we did without the help of dozens and dozens of undergraduate students, graduate students, parents, and babies who joined our Baby Signs® team over the years. So, whenever you read the words, "We found that . . .," keep in mind that it's a much bigger "we" than just the two of us.

Phase I: In the Beginning....

In the beginning there was a little, 12-month-old girl named Kate. She was (and still is!) Linda's daughter who, on a lovely summer's day in 1982, was so eager to communicate that she invented a sign. Linda never tires of telling the story:

> *Kate and I were in the garden behind our house like we had been so many times that summer. Suddenly, she turned to me with a grin on her face, pointed across the yard at a rose bush, and*

began sniffing. It didn't take a genius to figure out what she had in mind, and I automatically said, "Oh! The flowers. Yes, let's go see the flowers." I lifted her up, carried her to the bush, and proceeded to do what I frequently did with flowers when we were out and about: I picked a rose, sniffed it myself, and then put it under Kate's nose to do the same.

At this point, although my interest was piqued, I was not overly excited until I noticed Kate continuing to use the sniffing gesture the rest of the day. She found flowers absolutely everywhere—on the wall paper, dining table, in books, on her pajamas—and took great pleasure in labeling every one of them with a prolonged sniff. Now, I was excited and actually wrote in my journal that night, "Katie did the cutest thing today!"

After that, we all watched Kate carefully and noticed her making up other signs for things she wanted to talk about. In each case she would "borrow" a motion she had learned to associate with the relevant word in the context of some kind of routine. For example, she created a hands-up-high sign for "big" based on the movement in the game, "How Big's the Baby?" and she rubbed her index fingers together as a sign for "spider" based on the movement she'd learned from the "Eency Weency Spider" song. In each case she was plugging a movement in where a word would have gone. In other words, she was signing!

Realizing Kate's interest in signs, we began to model other simple signs for her. Given that, at that time, we had no background in formal sign languages like American Sign Language (ASL), these signs took the form of whatever movements made sense—scratching under the arms for MONKEY, bouncing for KANGAROO, etc. Kate soaked them up like a sponge and used them effectively until words burst forth at 17 months. We all had a fabulous time with the signing, including Kate.

She was thrilled to be able to get her messages across, and we were amazed at the window into her little mind we had gained.[2]

BABY SIGNS® STORY

"Where Oh Where Can He Be?"

Anna and James were among six babies having great fun learning signs with their moms at a local Sign, Say & Play™ Class. Like all of the babies, they had fallen in love the very first day with BeeBo™, the big Baby Signs® bear puppet that helped Mary, the instructor, teach all the classes. On this particular day, the fifth in the set of six classes, Mary had gotten caught in traffic and was late arriving. As a consequence, when Anna and James entered the classroom, BeeBo™ was nowhere in sight—a fact that was immediately made clear to Anna when James, after looking in vain around the room, toddled over to Anna

and signed BEAR with a quizzical look on his face.
Not to be outdone, Anna matched his sign with
a BEAR sign of her own—followed by her own
observation: ALL GONE! Needless to say, their
moms were speechless with delight.

Phase II: Starting the Search

At this point, we began searching the language development literature to see if others had documented such behavior. When we couldn't find anything, we decided we would fill in the gap with our own research. And so began the two decades of careful study designed to find out what the effect such signing behavior might have on infant development.

As we alluded to earlier, one of our discoveries was that Kate wasn't alone—that most babies spontaneously make up one or more signs on their way to talking.[3] Mother Nature has obviously built into babies not only the desire to communicate with those they love, but also a way to do so until their mouths catch up with their motivation!

We also discovered, however, that many parents were actually reluctant to encourage such behavior. Here's what we kept hearing over and over again from the parents we interviewed: "Won't communicating like this end up discouraging my baby from learning to talk?" Clearly, we had to find out.

Phase III: NIH-Funded Experimental Study

To do so, we applied for a grant from the National Institutes of Health and in 1989 launched a study of 11-month-old babies whose development we followed systematically for the next two years, that is, until they turned 3. What makes this longitudinal study so decisive is the fact that we divided the babies into groups, one group encouraged to use signs while the rest were not, and then compared the groups in terms of their average rates of language and cognitive development. A total of 103 families stayed with us to the end of the study. Here are some highlights:

> **Step 1**: **Baseline Assessment.** The first step was to make sure the groups were the same to begin

with in terms of factors known to affect language development. The factors we checked included gender, first- vs. later-born status, mother's education, father's education, income, and number of words already being spoken. As an additional check on general interest in communicating, we measured the amount of babbling each baby did during the initial visit to our lab. The groups did not differ significantly on any of these dimensions, thereby providing reassurance that any differences we might see at the end of the study wouldn't be due to differences present at the beginning of the study.

Step 2: Visits to the Lab. Each family visited our lab individually when their child was 15-, 19-, 24-, 30-, and 36-months-old. On each visit, we used standard language assessments designed to measure language comprehension (ability to understand words) and language production (ability to speak words). At 24 months, we also measured the children's ability to put words together into sentences and their intellectual development.

Step 3: The Results. The results were very clear, and the news was all good. On 16 of 17 language measures, the signing group's average scores were higher than the main control group's. More specifically, at 24 months of age, the signing children were on average talking more like 27- or 28-month-olds, representing more than a three-month advantage over the non-signing control group. In addition, the signing children were putting together significantly longer sentences and had scored higher on a standard measure of early intellectual development, the Bayley Mental Development Index. By 36 months, the signing children were talking more like 47-month-olds, putting them almost a full year ahead of their average age-mates. Similar advantages were also found on the language comprehension measures.

It's also important to point out that toddler boys were just as willing and able to use signs as toddler girls, in contrast to the slower development of boys compared to girls when it comes to saying words. The reason this is helpful for parents to know is because the frustration that toddler boys feel at having to wait longer to be able to talk often leads to aggression and tantrums. Having signs to use as they wait for their verbal skills to emerge helps boys avoid lashing out in frustration.

Conclusion. The data are clear. Families need have no worries that using signs will impede their child's early language or intellectual development. In fact, using signs appears to actually facilitate development in these important domains.[4]

WHAT SIGNING PARENTS SAY

At the time my daughter was born, signing was the new trend and so I tried it. She would get so frustrated sometimes and cry, and I didn't know why until she started learning signs. Her personality changed to a much happier baby! She had been frustrated that she couldn't tell us what she wanted or needed. What a difference it made for her to be able to communicate with signs and take charge of her surroundings! To this day, her language skills are exceptional, and I attribute this to her early language skills using signs. Doctors are always commenting on the maturity of her dialog compared to her peers. I truly think that she had a head start in her language because of the Baby Signs® Program.

–New Hampshire Mom

Phase IV: Looking for Long-Term Benefits.

Whenever we would report these data in the years following completion of the study, we would inevitably be asked, "And what about the long-term? Do these advantages continue as the children get older?" We had to say that we didn't know—and we usually added that we would be amazed if they did! After all, how could something that happens so early for such a comparatively short period of time (6-12 months until words burst forth) make a lasting difference? Finally, we had heard the question so often that we decided we'd better just go ahead and find out.

To this end, we located as many of the original children as we could at age 8 and assessed their language and intellectual development using the standard IQ test called the Wechsler Intelligence Scale for Children-III. Much to our surprise and delight, even all these years later, the children who had signed as babies were continuing to excel. With an average IQ score of 114 (75th percentile), the signing group had significantly out-performed the non-signing control group children by 12 points (Mean =

102, 53rd percentile).[5] Clearly, the language and cognitive advantage that the signing children had experienced early in their lives had provided a helpful "jumpstart" that just kept the ball rolling in a very positive direction!

Why is Signing so Helpful?

The next question that we are inevitably asked when people hear the results of our study is "Why?" Why does the act of signing have such a beneficial effect on learning to talk? There are at least four reasons.

1. **Increases Parent Language.** We've known for a long time that talking to babies, even though they can't yet answer back, helps babies learn to talk. Well, when babies use signs to point out things in the world or things they need, adults "flood" them with words in response. For example, if a baby signs CAT, how do adults usually respond? We say, "That's right! You see a kitty cat, don't you? Do you like that kitty?" Responses like these give babies lots of opportunities to learn words. What's more, babies tend to pay particularly close attention under these circumstances

because they have chosen the topic!

2. **Increases Motivation.** The success babies have getting their needs met with signs shows them how satisfying it is to be able to communicate effectively and motivates them to figure out even better ways to do so. The flood of verbal language around them makes clear that words are the way to go and they eagerly tackle the hard work of learning them. The way we like to make this point is by reminding parents about the relationship between crawling and walking. When babies learn to crawl, it doesn't slow down their interest in learning to walk; in contrast, it excites them about learning how to get around even better. Similarly, when babies learn to sign, it only excites them about communicating and motivates them to learn to do so even more effectively—with words. That's why we like to say . . . "Signing is to talking as crawling is to walking."

3. **Increases Interest in Books.** The ability to use signs increases a baby's interest in reading books by enabling the child to take an active role in naming things as the pages get turned. As is often the case, it's much more fun to actually participate than to just sit passively and listen. The positive effect on learning to talk comes from the fact that book-reading exposes children to more language from adults as well as opportunities to engage in a dialogue with other people about the book. Both factors foster language development.

BABY SIGNS® STORY

"Where There's a Will There's a Way"

Two toddlers, one from Israel and one from Taiwan, were best friends at their child care center. Despite the fact that neither one spoke nor understood the other's native language, they still found a way to enjoy a book together. Sitting on the floor with the book between them, one would turn the page, point at a picture, and the other would make the sign!

4. **Promotes Neurological Connections.** When a baby is successful using signs, connections get established between cells in the brain, thereby creating and strengthening circuits that then are available as the child moves on to learn words. Learning to talk is easier, in other words, because much of the work is already done. For example, a child who signs BIRD whenever he sees a bird and hears Mom reply, "You're right! It is a BIRD," is firming up connections in his brain between the object he's seeing and the word his mother is saying. All that's left is simply adding his own version of the word as soon as he can.

Whatever mixture of these reasons accounts for the positive impact of signing on verbal language for a particular child, the bottom line is that encouraging a baby to use signs is actually a wonderful way to help that baby achieve the ultimate goal—learning to talk.

CHAPTER 4

WHY THE BABY SIGNS®
PROGRAM IS SO POPULAR

Parents are always pleased to learn that the Baby Signs®
Program has such positive effects on language and
intellectual development, but that's generally not why
they rave about the program to friends and relatives.
Much more important to them are the many, many ways
in which signing makes daily life with baby both easier
and sweeter. Here are a few of the most important
benefits that parents in our research studies, as well as
parents who have read our books and attended Sign, Say
& Play™ classes, cite when they describe life with a baby
who uses signs.

Signing Reduces Frustration

By the time babies are 9 to 10 months old, they are quite capable of knowing what it is they need or want. What they don't know is how to tell us with words—which leads directly to frustration for baby and parent alike. All this changes when a baby is able to use signs. With signs like DRINK for thirsty, EAT for hungry, HOT and COLD—and many, many others—at their disposal, babies can make their needs known quickly and quietly without resorting to tantrums and tears. No wonder "Decreased frustration!" is the answer we most frequently get when we ask how signing has changed daily life.

Here's an example that shows how a baby's ability to sign can make a babysitter's job less frustrating too:

> The babysitter thought she'd gotten 15-month-old Grace down for the night, but suddenly she heard her crying. Going into her room, she saw Grace doing the BLANKET sign and turning her palms up to ask "Where is it?"—a gesture we all use. The babysitter started looking and, sure enough, discovered Grace's favorite

blanket lodged between the crib and the wall. "Oh, I bet this is what you're looking for," said the babysitter. Grace's smile as she clutched the newly retrieved blanket said it all.

But what if Grace hadn't had the sign? With the blanket so far out of sight that even Grace didn't have a clue where it was, who knows how long it would have taken the sitter to figure out the problem.

WHAT SIGNING PARENTS SAY

OK, so I thought that the concept for this book was a little out there. Signing with babies? But after dealing with what seemed like my 15-month-old daughter's 100th tantrum, I gave it a try. I kid you not, within ONE day (yes, one) she was using 3-4 of the signs! I was amazed and am now a believer! It's been about a month, and she is now using the words as well as the signs for words. The best part is that her temper has diminished because she's not so frustrated anymore! Neither are we!

—Massachusetts Mom

Signing Lets Babies Share Their World With Those They Love

Just because babies don't talk doesn't mean they aren't paying attention to the world around them. Babies are seeing things, thinking things, even remembering things, and with signs at their command, all this needn't remain their secret. Parents of signing babies are frequently amazed when their baby points out something using a sign that they never would have guessed she was even aware of. Not only do such occurrences increase parents' respect for their baby, they also help parents see the world through their baby's eyes and appreciate in a whole new way what an amazing world it is! Here's an example:

> During a visit with her aunt's family, Abby's port-a-crib was set up in her 4-year-old cousin's room. That night, her dad had finished tucking her into bed, had turned off the light, and was about to close the door when he heard Abby squeal. He turned the light back on, went back in, and found Abby signing STAR. Her dad looked around in vain and said, "I'm afraid I don't

see any stars, sweetheart," as he tucked her back in bed. But then, glancing back into the room as he once again turned out the light, he suddenly realized what Abby had been trying to tell him. Her cousin's ceiling was covered with florescent stars! Invisible with the lights on, the stars appeared as if by magic as soon as they were out. "You're right! There are stars!" he said, giving Abby a huge smile and a warm hug. The matching grin on Abby's face was a sure "sign" that she was thrilled she had been able to share this discovery with her dad.

Signing Strengthens the Parent-Infant Bond

Research shows that the main factor predicting whether a baby will feel loved and secure in her relationship with a parent is the number of positive interactions relative to the number of negative interactions they have. Several factors contribute to this equation.

First, babies depend on their parents to recognize when they need something and, secondly, to meet those needs in a timely fashion. Unfortunately, as every parent eventually learns, the first requirement can be difficult in and of itself. Because babies can't talk, it's often difficult to figure out what exactly they need. A parent's heart may be in the right place, but if she can't figure out why her baby is crying, she's not going to be as effective in supplying the comfort the baby is looking for. Because, as we said above, signs enable babies to communicate more specifically what's going on with them—what exactly they need to feel better—parents of signing babies are more likely to be able to meet those needs quickly and effectively, thereby increasing the probability of a stronger bond between them.

Second, like all of us, babies love those with whom they share good times. Signing comes into play because, as we pointed out above, being together is a lot more fun when baby and parent can truly understand each other. When they have signs to use, even very young children can "tell" their parents that they just saw an airplane, that they hear a dog barking, or that a bird just flew away. They can let their parents know whether they are happy, sad, or even afraid. In other words, life with a signing baby becomes a shared life—and with greater sharing comes a stronger, sweeter parent-infant bond. Here's an example:

Fifteen-month-old Samuel was settled in his father's arms on the back porch, both of them swaying gently back and forth in the comfy glider as dusk turned to darkness. Suddenly, Samuel turned to his father with a huge smile on this face and enthusiastically signed LIGHT, LIGHT. Searching the darkness beyond the porch, he quickly figured out what Samuel had seen: Fireflies! "You're right! I see them too!" said his Dad, both of them enjoying the magic moment.

WHAT SIGNING PARENTS SAY

I'm a language development specialist and an English teacher, and I love to see the way this method encourages formation of language concepts in my baby's mind. She's been "saying" three word sentences since 13 months, and the level of bonding and reduction of "what-does-that-baby-need" stress has been remarkable.

–California Mom

Signing Helps Parents Realize How Smart Their Babies Are

We can't tell you the number of times we've heard an astonished parent say, "I had no idea he was that smart!" Unfortunately, without words to tell us what they are thinking, babies have a hard time letting their parents know how much is really going on inside their heads. The truth is that they are busily thinking about what's going on around them, and with signs, they can finally let us know. Signs let us know that they are comparing and contrasting things ("Yes, you're right! Those street lights *do* look like the moon!"), remembering things ("Yep, we *did* see a pig when we were here last month!"), and empathizing with others ("You're right. Stephie *is* sad and *does* need a nap.").

Even conscientious parents can't always predict what signs their babies might enjoy. Fortunately, babies sometimes step in to the breach with their own sign creations. Here's an example that came to us from one of our Certified Baby Signs® Instructors:

> Little Lydia loved trying to swat flies with the fly swatter. Concerned about the unsanitary nature of the swatter, Mom decided to put it away. That didn't deter Lydia from asking for it, however, even though her mom had never thought to model a sign for "flyswatter." The next day Lydia confronted her mother with a three-sign combination: WHERE? + FLY + WATER. What was Lydia trying to say? You probably guessed quicker than Lydia's mom did: "WHERE'S THE FLY-s-WATER!"

Signing enhances infant self-esteem

What self-esteem boils down to for any of us is the sense that we are perceived as competent and praiseworthy in both our own eyes and in the eyes of those we love. And that's just what the ability to use signs yields. Because they can 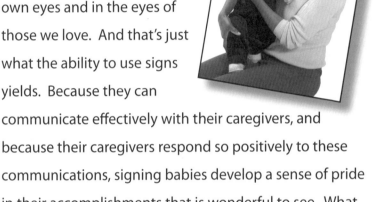 communicate effectively with their caregivers, and because their caregivers respond so positively to these communications, signing babies develop a sense of pride in their accomplishments that is wonderful to see. What better gift could you give your baby?

MORE GOOD NEWS!

Can signing benefit more than just middle-class families? Absolutely, according to a recent study in an Early Head Start program in Northern California conducted by Dr. Claire Vallotton of Harvard University. Dr. Vallotton compared parent-child interaction styles in families who were introduced to the Baby Signs® Program and families who were not. The results were very positive. Data from videotaped interactions and standard questionnaires indicated that . . .

- Mothers in the signing families perceived their children as more "reinforcing" and "acceptable," thus indicating more positive feelings toward their children.

- Mothers in the signing families were more "tuned in" to their children's emotions.

- Children in the signing families made more attempts to communicate with their mothers and expressed less distress.

Although only a first step, these promising results suggest that the addition of signing to the Early Head Start curriculum would be of benefit to families whose incomes or circumstances put them and their children in need of social services. (Paper presented at Zero to Three National Training Institute, Washington, DC, November 2005.)

.

CHAPTER 5
WHEN TO
START SIGNING

Probably the question parents ask most frequently
is about timing. Specifically, what's the best age to
start modeling signs for their baby? The answer is that
there's no "perfect" time to start signing. Over the years,
we've noticed three different approaches parents take
to the issue of when to get started. Each has its own
advantages. It's up to you to decide which approach will
work best for your family.

Birth – 8 months

Some parents start early—at birth or sometime during the first 8 months. These parents want their babies to get lots of exposure to both signs and words from the very beginning. They also like getting into the habit of signing early on. If you know that you have the patience and the persistence to use signs yourself even though your baby is unlikely to sign back until she's a bit older, then starting early may be a good choice for you.

8 – 12 months

Many parents choose to wait until their babies are 8-12 months old to start signing. The advantage of starting during this time period is that babies are closer to the age that they can start using signs themselves. If you like to see more immediate results, starting during this age range may be best for you.

12+ months

Some parents wait until their babies are 12-18 months old before they start using signs. Even at these later ages, most babies still don't have the words to express all the thoughts they want to share. The advantage of starting during this time is that babies are likely to learn signs more quickly, sometimes within a matter of days. With this approach, however, babies will use their signs for a shorter length of time because signs drop off quickly once babies start using more spoken words.

Here's the most important point to remember: any baby or toddler who shows readiness to communicate, but cannot do so effectively with words, is a candidate for signing, and as a parent, you should not feel that it's too early *or too late* to start.

If two or more of the following accurately describe your baby, it's time to start signing:

- Is your baby beginning to point to things?

- Is your baby bringing toys or objects to you and looking for a response?

- Is your baby beginning to wave "bye-bye"?

- Is your baby beginning to shake his/her head for "no" or "yes"?

- Is your baby beginning to take an interest in picture books?

- Does your baby knows a few words, but can't yet talk about lots of important things?

When Will Your Baby Begin Signing Back?

How soon your baby starts signing back to you depends not only on developmental readiness (as indicated by the behaviors listed above), but also on:

1. How often you demonstrate the signs you're trying to teach, and . . .

2. How interested your baby is in communication.

Being consistent about signing will help your baby learn faster. However, even when parents are signing consistently, babies don't start signing until they are good and ready! Just as with crawling, walking, or teething, every baby has his or her own unique developmental timetable, and it's important to respect that. For example, some babies are much more interested in developing their motor skills than in communicating. Moms of babies like this often put it in these terms, "My baby is more interested in climbing the bookshelves than in reading the books!"

But even though your baby isn't signing back yet, it doesn't mean that your efforts are going unnoticed. In fact, well before babies produce their first signs, they watch their parents' actions carefully and begin comprehending what those actions represent. You can observe this understanding by making a sign for an object in the vicinity of your baby and seeing if your baby turns to look at it.

So, be patient and keep modeling signs. We guarantee that the proud smile on your baby's face after he's made his first sign WILL be worth the wait!

CHAPTER 6
HOW TO CHOOSE
AND TEACH SIGNS

Regardless of when you start signing, choosing the
best signs for your baby will help to ensure her signing
success. Like all of us, babies are most likely to learn
something when they care about it. That principle
should guide your choice of signs. The more important
an object or event is to your baby's life, the more
likely he is to communicate with you about it and,
therefore, pay attention to what you're doing. Here are
some more specific guidelines to help you make your
choices:

1. **Choose from among nouns, verbs, and describing words.** These tend to be the most salient kinds of words for babies and are typical of early vocabularies. Babies love to sign about "objects" like their toys, animals, and food. They also enjoy signs about things they love to do, like "play," "eat," and "love." And finally, they appreciate being able to use descriptors, like "hot," "big," and "all gone."

2. **Choose signs for items for which your child does not yet say the word.** Remember, a main goal of teaching signs is to help children communicate when they don't have a verbal way to express thoughts and desires.

3. **Choose signs for items that allow for frequent use throughout the day.** The more you have an opportunity to practice modeling and eliciting signs, the easier it will be for your baby to learn to sign back to you. Choosing signs from daily routines like mealtime, bedtime, bath time, and

your family routines (park, car rides, trips to school) is a great way to help you and your baby have many chances for signing adventures!

4. **Make a list of your baby's favorite things, including books, toys, animals, foods, people, and objects.** For example, if your baby is fascinated by balls, then the BALL sign is a natural. If your baby loves bananas, then the BANANA sign is a good choice. Or if your baby loves the book *Goodnight Moon* by Margaret Wise Brown, then think about teaching the BUNNY, MOON, and MOUSE signs. You get the idea.

And remember, no matter which signs you choose to introduce, be on the lookout for signs your baby may invent all by himself!

How to Teach a Sign

Teaching your baby the signs for BIRD, EAT or HURT is actually no different than teaching her to wave her hand when someone goes out the door. That's why we like to say . . . "Signing with babies is as easy as waving bye-bye!"

And what exactly is it that we do to teach "bye-bye?" First, there's an event that makes saying "bye-bye" appropriate—like Grandma leaving. Next, we get the baby's attention and say something like, "Look, Morgan, Grandma's leaving." Then, as we say the words, "Say BYE-BYE! BYE-BYE Grandma!" with great emphasis, we wave our own hand in an exaggerated manner, perhaps even gently wave the baby's hand. Eventually, after the baby has witnessed enough of these episodes, the light bulb comes on and she waves bye-bye herself (although, admittedly, at first it's usually after Grandma is gone!). Teaching signs is that easy. Let's try it out with the sign for MORE. Here's the situation: Little Morgan is sitting in her high chair and has just stuffed the last piece of banana into her mouth.

Step 1: You get her attention.

Step 2: You say, "Morgan, would you like some MORE banana? Are you still hungry? Would you like some MORE?"

Step 3: Every time you say the word "more" you also model the MORE sign—which is merely tapping the fingertips of both hands together.

Now, you may or may not have guessed correctly about Morgan still feeling hungry. The point is only that you have started to teach Morgan that when she does want "more" of something, she can let you know by tapping her fingertips together as you did. Repeat this consistently whenever you say the word "more" to her, and eventually she'll catch on.

Similarly, if it's the CAT sign that you're teaching, you simply model the sign (tracing whiskers on your cheek) every time you notice a cat—whether real, toy, or a picture in a book—always pairing the word and sign together.

Within a day or two you'll find it becoming so natural to pair the word and sign together that you won't even have to think about it!

SIGNING AND SIBLINGS

Worried about your older child feeling jealous of the newcomer in the house? Although it isn't a total cure, the Baby Signs® Program actually helps soothe those ruffled feathers. Older siblings take enormous pleasure in teaching signs to their little brother or sister. For example, one mom reported that her 5-year-old found magazine pictures of whatever sign he was trying to teach the baby (CAT, for example), posted them all over the house, and made the rounds with the baby, modeling the sign at each stop. However an older sibling achieves it, the

pride that's felt when baby starts to use a sign herself
makes big brother or sister feel like a partner with
Mom and Dad—as a part of the Baby Signs® Team.

Ten Tips for Signing Success

Based on our decades of helping parents teach their babies to sign, we've come up with a list of strategies that really increase the chance that a family will have a successful signing experience. Here they are:

1. **Start with just a few.** Like many parents, you're probably eager for your baby to learn lots of signs. That's great! But the way to go about it is not to start modeling lots of signs right off the bat. Instead, we suggest that you start with a few, perhaps as few as two or three. The reason we make this suggestion is not because teaching too many signs at once will overload your baby. It's really just to help you keep track of which signs you're trying to teach so that you'll remember to model them consistently.

So, what are some good signs with which to start your signing adventure? Because even very young babies are highly motivated to communicate about food and drink, the following make excellent starter signs:

| Milk | More | Eat | Drink | All Done |

Babies are also drawn to animals, especially if there's a pet in the home. In such cases, a sign for the relevant animal (e.g., CAT or DOG) can be an excellent sign to start with, too.

WHAT SIGNING PARENTS SAY

I had heard of using sign language with babies and was very interested in trying it out with my newborn son. Around 7 months we started with various mealtime and animal signs. Then a few weeks later he displayed his first sign: FISH! Every time he passed his beloved pets in their watery home he

would squeal and start smacking his little lips. I
was overjoyed! He soon followed with ALL DONE,
HELLO/GOODBYE and MORE. At 9.5 months I
was even more impressed when he made up his own
sign for PHONE. There is no end to my amazement
at how much this little guy is capable of!

–Michigan Mom

2. **Always use the sign and the word together.** The
ultimate goal for typically-developing children is to
learn to say words. The signs in this case are mainly a
stop-gap measure to minimize frustration until words
are available. When babies hear their parents say a
word, they begin to mentally register and remember
the sequence of sounds—an important step in learning
to say the word themselves. By always adding the
word to the sign, you are making it easier for your baby
to eventually produce the word himself.

3. **Repeat the sign and word several times.** Repetition
is the key to learning anything, and signs are no
exception. The more a baby sees a sign, the easier it

is for her to figure out what it stands for and how to make it. The repetition we're talking about here is within a single situation. For example, when you ask your baby if she would like some more, say "more" and make the sign MORE at the same time. Do this several times in a row. Such repetition will help your baby identify exactly which word is the one that the sign represents.

4. **Point when possible.** If the sign you are teaching stands for an object (for example, DOG), try pointing to the object as you are saying the word and making the sign. This is a very easy habit to establish because you probably already point to things when labeling them with words alone. Remember, you are actually asking your child to make a three-way connection: (1) sign to object, (2) word to object, and (3) sign to word. Pointing makes the connection easier for your baby to detect.

5. **Gently guide your baby's hands.** When it seems helpful, gently manipulate your baby's hands to help him get the feel of the motion. But keep in mind that

babies can also be pretty independent at times. Some babies like help, while others prefer to do it on their own. So, pay close attention to your baby's response to make sure your help is welcome.

6. **Make signing a part of your daily activities.** As we've said before, repetition is the key to success. One way to remember to model the signs you're trying to teach your baby is to incorporate reminders into your daily routines. Teaching the CAT sign? Place kitty stickers on your baby's high chair and/or bib so you're reminded to model the signs at mealtime. Teaching the FROG sign? Add a plastic frog to the bath tub. Be creative, and you'll find yourself easily providing the repetition your baby needs. As we point out in Tip #10, teaching signs should become a natural part of daily interactions, not the focus of rigid "lesson times."

BABY SIGNS® STORY

"Some Food for Thought"

*Susan's granddaughter, 14-month-old Emma,
was seated with all her aunts, uncles, and
cousins around the big dining room table. It was
Thanksgiving, and the table was covered with dishes
of food, everything from applesauce to zucchinis.
As everyone began to dig in, Emma turned to Amy,
her mom, and signed EAT. "What do you want,
Emma? Some peas?" Emma shook her head "no."
In fact, she continued to shake her head "no" as her
mom tried three more suggestions. Then suddenly,
as though she had just remembered, Emma grinned
and signed CHEESE. "Oh! You want some
cheese!" said Amy and went to the kitchen to get
it. But what if Emma hadn't had the sign? Amy
could have systematically tried every other food on
the table and still not have gotten it right! Because
of the sign, Emma got what she wanted and both
Emma and her mom enjoyed the satisfaction of
understanding each other rather than the frustration
of not being able to communicate.*

7. **Watch for opportunities.** As you go about the world with your baby, be on the look-out for examples of the things the signs you are teaching your baby represent. Books, DVDs, and outings to the circus, the zoo, farms, or even the grocery store can provide great opportunities to practice signs.

As you'll see when you and your baby watch the *My Baby Signs*® DVD that accompanies this book, all the modeling need not come from you. Using state-of-the art animation, BeeBo™, and real babies to model the signs, we've designed not only this DVD, but all the other Baby Signs® DVDs, to help your baby learn signs simply in the course of being entertained.

You'll find that most of the specific signs on the My Baby Signs® DVD (DOG, CAT, DUCK, BOOK, HAT, and ALL GONE[6]) are also included in the board books you've received. Such overlap ensures even more repetition.

8. **Be flexible.** Remember, the main goal of signing with your baby is to improve communication between you and your baby. If your baby makes up a sign and you

understand it, feel free to use it even if it's not one that we've suggested. The decision about what signs to use is totally up to you.

It's also important to remember that few babies will be able to produce the signs in precise imitation of the way you model them. Their limited motor skills often preclude detailed movements, and attempts to insist on perfection will backfire, making your baby less, rather than more, interested in trying to sign.

9. **Be patient.** Remember, all babies are unique, with individual temperaments and timetables. Just because your neighbor's baby is already signing at 10 months doesn't mean your baby should be doing so, too. Also remember, the younger your baby, the longer it will take him to begin producing signs on his own.

10. **Make learning signs FUN!** The Baby Signs® Program is not about "lesson times" or demanding a sign before granting a child what he or she needs; it's about making signs a natural part of everyday interactions

with your baby. Keep in mind that babies who feel pressured, tired, or frightened are unlikely to respond positively to anything. Happiness and signing make a two-way street: happy babies are more likely to learn signs, and learning signs is likely to make for a happier baby!

CHAPTER 7

WHAT TO EXPECT
ALONG THE WAY

An Important Corner Your Baby May Turn

The corner we have in mind here is the shift from using single words or signs to putting them together into 2-word (or sign) sentences. For children who do not use signs, this milestone occurs on average between 19 and 20 months. Instead of just saying "Daddy" when they see their father drive away, now they say "Daddy bye-bye," or instead of just saying "cookie," now they can say "More cookie."

The lovely thing is that children who use signs begin putting words together at earlier ages—and begin putting signs together earlier still! There are two kinds of combinations to watch for:

- SIGN + SIGN: asking for more milk with the signs MORE + MILK, or

- SIGN + "Word": asking for more milk with the sign MORE + the word "milk."

Certain signs are especially likely to be included in such fledgling sentences because they are easily combined with lots of other words and signs. These popular candidates for combinations include MORE, ALL DONE, WHERE IS IT? and BYE-BYE.

Consider, for example, just a few of the things that can be combined with ALL DONE:

- ALL DONE + BOOK when the last page of a bed-time book has been turned.

- ALL DONE + AIRPLANE when the airplane disappears into the clouds.

- ALL DONE + DOG
  when the family dog
  has finished his dinner.

So, watch for the start of little sentences like these—and even longer ones—as a "sign" of your baby having turned a very important corner in language development.

WHAT SIGNING PARENTS SAY

I used the Baby Signs® Program with my son (who is now 6) beginning at about 10 months of age. He caught on right away—we began with animal signs/sounds—and by 1 year of age he was combining signs with simple words to make "sentences." He even began making up signs of his own to describe things. It was amazing to be able to "converse" with my son before he could talk. When we would walk through the mall, he would look for things he knew how to sign (e.g., a stuffed fish in a toy store display) and would get so excited that I could acknowledge what he was seeing. I truly believe that he gained a lot of confidence by being able to communicate with me so early.

–Pennsylvanian Mom

The Inevitable Transition

As much fun as signing is, we certainly want our babies to move on to words. Fortunately, we don't have to worry about that happening. Babies are irresistibly drawn to talking. All over the world, no matter how much signing they do or don't do, children eventually learn first to say single words, then to put them together into sentences, and then to put sentences together into full conversations—and on and on and on.

As we've explained many times, the Baby Signs® Program is designed as an interim step on the way to this verbal progression. The simple signs we suggest work for a while, but as babies turn into toddlers and then into young preschoolers, things change and they find they need the more complex options that speech provides. Here are a few of the changes that spur them on to conquering verbal language:

- **New places to go.** As toddlers get more mobile, they revel in the opportunity to explore their worlds, often at some distance from mom and dad—perhaps even out of sight. And if a baby is too far away or can't see his parent, there's not much use in signing! In contrast, words can be heard around corners and across playgrounds.

- **New faces to meet.** When babies are young, the number of people they meet in a given day is relatively small. But as they get older and move around on their own, they are destined to meet more and more people who don't recognize their signs—but who would understand words.

- **New things to say.** To a 15-month-old, simply telling you that he sees a butterfly is a magnificent feat. In such cases, a single sign will do. However, as children grow intellectually, the ideas they want to get across become much more complicated. Instead of just mentioning the butterfly, he may want to say that this butterfly is like the one he saw yesterday, or that he knows it came from a cocoon, or that its colors remind him of Halloween. Ideas of this complexity—unless the child has parents who are fluent in a formal sign language—require more than the simple signs we emphasize in the Baby Signs® Program.

BABY SIGNS® STORY

"An Explosion of Words!"

Parents who are worried that their toddler seems to be taking a long time to begin talking can take heart from Linda's experience with her son, Kai.

At 19 months, Kai was quite the signer with a vocabulary of over 40 signs. However, his verbal vocabulary had stayed stuck at 7 words for months. Mom was confident that words would eventually come along, but she wasn't prepared for the rapidity with which it happened! Suddenly, the dam broke and between 19 and 20 months, Kai added 67 new words! The signing had clearly helped him get everything ready so that when he finally could say words, all he needed was to add the sounds to the wealth of information he'd already gained through signing.

What the Transition Looks Like

Even though we often get the impression that babies make great intellectual leaps between the time they go to bed at night and the time they get up in the morning, when it comes to the shift from signs to words, the process is usually much more gradual. Once in a while, it's true, we'll see a word appear out of nowhere, and—poof!—the sign is gone. But in the majority of cases the transition goes like this:

1. Sign alone

2. Sign + word together

3. Word alone

The point at which babies combine a sign with its word is actually very helpful to parents because the sign can help clarify what the baby is trying to say. The baby who says "Bah" could be trying to say *baby*, *bottle*, or *ball*. If she adds the BALL sign, the mystery is solved.

But finally the signs do disappear, although they may reappear occasionally when babies are eating and their mouths are full, when they are in church and are supposed to be quiet, or for added emphasis when a parent isn't paying attention to their words.

CHAPTER 8

YOU'RE ON YOUR WAY!

Now that you've come to the end of this overview of the Baby Signs® Program, all that's left is to start your own signing adventure. As you begin putting into practice the advice we've provided, remember that help is available from our network of Certified Baby Signs® Instructors. They can answer questions, suggest additional resources, and offer you the opportunity to meet other families interested in signing through their Parent Workshops and Sign, Say & Play™ classes. Check our website to find an instructor in your area.

Also remember that by helping your baby learn to sign before he can talk, you are giving him a gift that will last a lifetime. By enabling your baby to connect with those he loves, express his emotions in constructive ways, and build a sense of being competent and valued, signs are helping lay a foundation that will make your baby stronger and better able to meet the many challenges that lay ahead in life.

At the same time you are giving yourself a gift as well. As you'll soon be discovering, your baby's ability to share her world with you through signing will yield some truly fascinating moments as you gaze with wonder through the magical window signing provides into your baby's mind.

Happy Signing!

Endnotes

[1] Other Baby Signs® Instructors are professionals, such as Speech Pathologists and Early Childhood Educators, who have seen the children in their care blossom both cognitively and emotionally from the ability to communicate effectively with signs before they could talk. All Certified Baby Signs® Instructors offer a wide variety of services and resources. Visit www.babysigns.com to locate an instructor near you.

[2] We kept careful records of Kate's verbal and nonverbal vocabularies through age 2 and published these data in the following peer-reviewed article: Acredolo, L.P., & Goodwyn, S.W. (1985). Symbolic gesturing in language development: A case study. *Human Development, 28*, 40-49.

[3] The details can be found in the following peer-reviewed paper: Acredolo, L. P. & Goodwyn, S. W. (1988). Symbolic gesturing in normal infants. *Child Development, 59*, 450-466.

[4] These data are available in the following peer-reviewed publication which is also available on our website, www.babysigns.com: Goodwyn, S.W., Acredolo, L.P., & Brown, C. (2000). Impact of symbolic gesturing on early language development. *Journal of Nonverbal Behavior, 24*, 81-103

[5] The peer-reviewed report of these data presented at the International Conference on Infant Studies in Brighton, England is available in full on our website, www.babysigns.com.

[6] Babies automatically use the concepts ALL GONE and ALL DONE interchangeably. That's why, in our products and packaging, you'll sometimes see the sign referred to as ALL GONE and other times as ALL DONE.